The One That Got Away

Graham Allen

Best wishes

Graham

29. v. 14

New Binary
Press

Published in 2014
by New Binary Press
Cork city, Ireland

www.newbinarypress.com

ISBN 978-0-9574661-9-7

For Carrie

Acknowledgements

With thanks to those editors who have previously published these poems in the following journals:

"Gravity", "Unrequited", and "Those Feet" in *Southword*
"Ack, Ack, Ack" and "Autunno" in *The Stinging Fly*
"Plenty More" in *The Rialto*
"A Night in with the Stars" in *Poetry Ireland Review*
"Auctioneer" in *Revival*
"Passage" in *The Salt Companion to Harold Bloom*
"Beyond Livy" (1 to 6) (with 'Mosul Journal' drawings by Steve Mumford) in *Cultural Politics*
"A Prayer" and "Here, Now, Blake" in *The SHOp*
"The Fags" in *Cyphers*
"Miss Universe", "I wouldn't start from here", "Transverse Myelitis", "Patrick Street", "On Thomas Butt's *A View of Cork*" and "Military Hill" in *The Weary Blues*
"Dreamhole" in *Transmission Annual 1*
"Evidence", "Stranieri", "To Geoffrey Hill", "Lago Trasimeno, July 2011", "Sortilege" and "Hung Over" in *The New Binary Press Anthology of Poetry: Volume I*

"The One That Got Away" won the 2010 Listowel Poetry Prize and was published in the festival's *Winners' Anthology 2013*.

An earlier version of this collection was shortlisted for the 2012 Crashaw Poetry Prize.

Contents

The One That Got Away

Lago Trasimeno

"During the time occupied in completing the drawing, the Flea told [Blake] that all fleas were inhabited by the souls of such men as were by nature blood-thirsty to excess, and were therefore providentially confined to the size and form of insects; otherwise, were he himself, for instance, the size of a horse, he would depopulate a great portion of the country."

> – John Varley, *A Treatise on Zodiacal Physiognomy* (1828), quoted in Alexander Gilchrist, *Life of William Blake: Pictor Ignotus* (1863)

The One That Got Away

I wouldn't start from here

I'd start from there, or there,
or over there, or anywhere,
really, but here. You see,
here is nowhere until
it's someone's somewhere
and it will never be that
until someone, you perhaps,
is somewhere else.
I was once somewhere else,
so I know what I'm about
and could not speak true,
as I do on this topic,
if I had not travelled
far out into the misty murk
of there, and over there,
many, many receding roads,
every circular one of which,
homewards, led me here.
These are my hill-top lights,
this is my moon,
my urban scream, my night-time dogs,
my comfortable, familiar rain.
Those who ask for directions
are clearly not at home
and, quite clearly then, logically,
should not start from here.

The One That Got Away

The only book he would read was *The Time Machine*,
the only colour he could stand was blue,
he boarded up the windows from the inside
and learned to find food like a cat in the garden.
He collected rain-water in baked-bean tins,
trained his eyes to negotiate the darkness.
Every morning, as regular as clock-work,
he made his poetic bid for freedom.
He wrote a poem about Blake and eternity,
when he flung it in the fire it curled like a trout.
He wrote a ballad about Orion as a pin-headed cybot,
then tore it into strips and ate it as pasta.
He wrote three hundred sonnets addressed to his father,
each one of them soggy enough to sip.
He wrote an epic about Ceres and her seasons,
stuffed into his duvet it warmed him during winter nights.
Finally he realized the answer had been there
all that long, long time inside of the moon,
so he sat on the grass by the rusting deck-chairs,
inside his overgrown, night-time garden,
slowed his eyes to the monthly ebb and flow,
construction and ruination of herself,
the breathing in and out of her diaphragm,
even kept faith with the fake, stony shape
she would pin up into the blue of the day,
until he had written the most original poem
anyone of his kind had ever penned.
By the time it was time to reopen doors and windows
his house was a bank with a security system.

Gravity

Nowadays I wonder at my memory,
which like the universe, they say,
has not enough dark matter, too little adhesive,
to keep things from slowly drifting apart.

So that what was once linked and logical,
places, buildings, lost friends, incidents,
stripped of all context, become lonely wanderers
that haunt me for reasons I cannot now retrieve.

As in those two towers I habitually connect.
The first, between Lockerbie and Elvanfoot,
where in his seventeenth-century estate
some Lord of the Manor I may have read up on

constructed for himself, out of a need
I remember all those years ago
said something to me, a place of complete
and utter seclusion, a Redemption Tower,

so called, in which, and this is what returns,
like a disturbing dream I cannot shake off,
he would sit, stripped of every distraction
save for the one sin he could not endure,

for weeks and weeks, his meals levered up
on an external dumb-waiter, until,
presumably, the god of his own mind
gave him Grace and permission to descend.

The other, on the eastern side of Scotland,
somewhere near the Sidlaw Hills,
where, with a work colleague, his wife
and their newborn child, no more than six months,

wrapped and cosseted in layers of wool,
what must have been forty feet in the air
of some old and generally neglected pile,
the icy terrain swept out before us,

vertigo grabbing me by the balls,
grinning at some joke, they offered me their child,
and I took it, in all my bachelor alarm,
as we continued to chat about work matters,

the news, gossip, the way it was conceived,
my own ridiculous sex life then. I forget,
but what matters, my memory, the thing
that bites me still, like the monster always there

in the corner of the eye, is that whilst they spoke,
happiness exemplified, I had such a need
to fling their baby over the edge,
to live its drop, and then ask them how they felt?

Unrequited

Someone that I loved and could not have,
and that slow, inexorable scenario
that does not return, because it never goes away.

Too methodical to be a nightmare,
wholly transparent in its meaning;
the one time my dark self simply brought a mirror.

She literally divided, unfolded,
it was not at all clear what she knew,
and I, and this is the thing, continuing.

No doubt there were residual traces,
previous entanglements involved;
but nothing significant enough to vindicate.

There could never be enough lost chances,
befuddled errors, radiant faces spitting betrayal,
to make a line of creditable defence.

Someone that I loved and could not have,
who did not want to accept the gift
of my life, priceless jewel that it was.

And so I said, "open up to me,"
knowing how shot through, how riddled and torn
she was, and I said, "I will make you whole."

The one time my dark self simply brought a mirror,
she literally divided, unfolded,
and I, and this is the thing, continuing.

Sortilege

Inspired by the *Sortes Vergilianæ*
we worked out a sign system
before she left for good:

two for *no*, three for *yes*, one for *be patient*,
simple combinations
for basic questions,

such as, *does anyone seem to know?*
or, *is it cold as they say?*
and, *have they given you directions?*

But after a while we entered
a chilled and windy season
and the world began to intrude.

I asked that one about pain
and punishment, and the windows
shook without meaning.

I asked whether we would be together,
a roof-slate smashed into pieces
and a stray-dog began to howl.

All through the visible world,
the answers she gave me
were scattering like leaves.

It was as if she were leaving me
and the house, driven out by noisy,
ignorant squatters.

In the end I was reduced to a single
query, repeated and repeated,
and answered, in a way:

a lone fly buzzing around the vegetables,
and, beyond the window,
two planes marking a wispy cross.

The Look

He looks inside her,
with a silent, inexpressive look,
his default face impenetrable.
He sees beyond her cheerfulness,
her melancholia,
the tears she shed last Christmas,
anxieties over children.
He looks within the sharp,
precise blade of her intelligence,
her neatly collected memories,
a thousand books, snaps of time,
relationships hung like reproductions,
passed the idol of herself
she cherishes and lets down,
her confident, sensual fingers.
He scans, as he wanders through,
her lifetime's photo gallery:
the father dead, brothers
at all ages, her mother's
uncomplaining smile, friends,
the unimportant lovers,
her life from infancy to now,
on beaches, in unfamiliar rooms,
overlooking foreign cities,
or rambling down from mountain tops
to all the unaging pints in bars.
He comes across faces he does not know,
younger, naïve, impatient, calm,
but he moves towards the open door
of her still unfulfilled desire.
The white light blinds him
to shapes that gather and depart,
the frantic jockeying of futurity,
the limit of what comes to view.

Transverse Myelitis

A fuse has blown in the refrigerator
of your spinal cord, Frida Kahloesque,
and slowly the meat and the butter are bleeding
onto the Roquefort, melon and water-cress.

Here, Now, Blake

Christological must have been,
for him, non-dative,
announcement made, first time,
as re-announcement,
then, there and always, so
no fall from innocence into sin
and back again, no then
and now and then, but only,
always, an angel in that tree
in Lambeth, a devil in the forecourt
of 13 Hercules Buildings, here, now
and always, in the moment
and not before, so that Lambeth,
where people walk and work,
kiss, kill and copulate,
collapses and begins again
without chronology, without
solidity of public name,
call it Lamb-berth, call it
lamb birth, his dreams
from his bed in Lambeth,
call it Bed Lamb, call
it Bedlam, call it Bed-
Lamb-Birth, mythologize,
word play, until heaven
and our mother-tongue
procreate beyond violence
and war and coalesce.

The Book of Job

i

Job knew God had stolen his face
and that it was transference,
projection, in the strictly Freudian sense,
that coloured his decision.
But what good was such knowledge?
The answer comes in four parts,
as he himself eventually understood.
The man who first made a mirror, first
part, deserves to be hung and quartered.
This is little less than obvious,
deprive such a man of reflection.
Evil is a concept created by skin, second
part. It was skin that invented
pain and the anthropomorphic
reproduction of same. This came
to Job on the news of his children,
his youngest daughter's eyes
had been characterised mirror-like.
He buried them in the sand, refused
to raise stone monuments
to a god drunk on speculation.
It took him a long time before the third
insight, his family butchered, his live-stock
razed, the foundations of his settlement
burnt and levelled, and, as we know,
the ultimate insult, time and time
again making him scream for annihilation.
Poor pot-boiled, pus-filled Job,
unable to stand or sit or sleep,
his body a metaphor for human history,
screaming for the nothingness
and the dignity of death, its sweet
relief from all division. This was
the last resuscitating lesson.

22

ii

When Sadar was born we could smell the flowers
wafted by hot draughts from the Judean hills.
I knew then that the worst would happen.
When we managed to unblock the doorway
into the bedroom, now open to the street,
we saw what looked like a rain-soaked coat
pinned up on a nail against the far wall.
The coat had no head, or say no hood,
that took a considerable time to find.
When we finally put the two together
the last piece of my heart fell into ruin.
They put Sadar into a black plastic bag
as the scent of frankincense and aloe
wafted in from the bedroom's empty wall.

The first word he said was mother,
he would crawl patiently towards my ankles.
When he stood without help I wept,
I knew that the worst would happen.
He liked chocolate milk and raisins,
his chuckle was like the summer sun.
He had his father's noble face
and all of his mother's aching heart.
I would have given him sisters,
to play with and adore him.
We marched him down our shattered street
and put his tiny box into the earth.
One week later the jets returned
and made a crater of his grave.

iii

At the end of Blake's illuminated book,
they line up once again,
the seven sons and three daughters
restored to their thankful parents.
Even the sheep are standing up,
trauma salved by sweet reunion.
And yet sometimes I look at her,
the wife, the mother, the silent witness,
and wonder what she really thinks
of these replicant daughters? Jemima,
Kezia, Keren-happuch, those fair,
much admired teetotal simulacra.
I scan her impassive, benign features
for signs of a quiet mourning,
her natural children murdered
on the whim of his childless God.

Ack! Ack! Ack!

In July in Via del Plebiscito
improbable sea-gulls begin at sun rise,
their ugly, mechanical, repetitious squawks
reminding me of my time in Scotland,
in the cities of its eastern coastline,
where in summer the sun hardly sets at all.
And, in turn, my mind goes back to Revelation
and the anti-Christ emerging from a city
of seven hills: Athens, Rome, Sheffield,
Aberdeen, Aberystwyth, the last
a place name I cannot quite pronounce.
And I wonder, in sleepless vigil,
whether, since that prophecy was made,
these tongue-tied scavengers have not been attempting
to stutter out their knowledge of the answer.

Memento Mori

Over time she grew restless.
The birds did not sing
so tunefully that summer.
She lost her appetite, her desire
to walk into town.
She let the garden go,
watched the houseplants droop
then give up the ghost,
heard knocks at the door
but did not move to answer.
The one remaining peach
in the Chinese-design fruit bowl
turned slowly blue
before imploding.
Gradually she realized
that she was being filmed
by a group of unfamiliar children
with hand-held video-cameras.
She thought about Italy,
the paint-blue sky,
and that boy who had hurled
her into the stars,
more than sixty years ago.
She took her pills, because
without them she couldn't think.
One by one, she separated
the family photographs
from their frames: the weddings,
the birthdays, the graduations,
strange houses
containing grandchildren,
that one of himself
on leave in Germany.
Day after day, in her chair
by the window, the nets
gently parted, she returned

26

to her Italian
and the language problem,
saw the medieval hills
and distant mountains
beyond Cortona, tasted
hand-made lemon ice-cream
at Castiglione del Lago.

Military Hill

What do you want?
What would you have wanted?

I see you sometimes in the street,
I did not mean to keep you unborn.

You are playing football.
You have brown eyes and a hurt nose.

You are running for your life.
I cannot help you.

From this distance you have no name.
You burn in the palm of my hand.

You stand, unseen, outside of every window.
We did not hear you calling,

or you yourself were deaf.
But we need you now,

Cork boy with matted hair,
a toy gun and torn trousers,

kicking cans down Military Hill,
madly excited about tomorrow.

On Thomas Butt's *A View of Cork*

If I had the skill of the painter
I would swivel the geography of Cork,
so that we did not separate each evening,
but walked home together, peaceful-like,
you to the south, me to the north.

The Elysian

Ghost factory,
high-rise imitation,
empty observatory.
The only occupants are resident tonight,
they have made two camp fires,
square eyes gazing northwards.
The blue haze of the television flickers,
tiny people in a fragile doll's house.
I see their shades
as they walk past sources of light.
The bedroom lamp is constant.

Above them a green fist,
one finger pointing at the moon.

Down the unpaced corridors,
out of untried locks and windows,
through unopened shopfronts,
down into the unviewed garden vista
flows the news about tomorrow.
The visionaries have all gone blind
under orange emergency strip lighting.

If you listen very carefully,
without motion, without breath,
you can almost hear the sound of children
playing in the elevators,
splashing in the sculptured rock pool,
plunging to their early deaths.

The Big House

March is a month for opening windows,
spring fastened onto the earth,
life erupting into the hillsides,
the nightmare of ice and darkness
a distant memory.
It was at that time of year
we decided to stay together,
put away our childish games,
and move into the big house.
Although He wasn't there,
that He had been was palpable:
the stairs were happy and smelled of wood again,
the dense intoxication of fir trees;
liberated birds sung above the kitchen grate
where the light sheeted in as sharp as glass.
Before we rearranged the chairs,
centred the long mahogany table,
dried and dabbed the lamps and windows,
I could feel my lungs expanding
with a fuller, easier air,
my hands sucking in the spirit of the place,
like steam into a vacuum.
I remember thinking: "So this is it.
The place in which we will write our best poems,
conceive our happiest children,
and make the most perfected love
this side of the angels' true bliss.
Here we will be prosperous.
We must abandon ourselves in every room,
wake this house up with human fire,
we must wear our most expensive clothes,
banish denial from the upper rooms
and then from the lower and then from the grounds."
"Before too long," I also thought,
with my talent for conjuring up the worst, "He'll be
horning his way home to surprise us."

Plenty More

She has gone and will not be coming back
and so, for my own good, they inform me
she was a fish of a very common variety.
I am told I should bypass mourning
because of her amphibian qualities.
But I loved the way she smelled, after sex,
of mackerel, or other as yet unnamed creatures,
the way her skin shone in the water,
her hair, made of luxurious, black sea-weed,
the way she plunged when others merely danced,
never once needing to break for air,
and that look I would catch in the oceans
of her pale blue eyes, that spoke of other seas,
the warmer, brighter worlds of which we dream.

Miss Universe

Nobody can teach you anything.
Your self-deprecation is a lie.
Always the first to highlight your own weakness,
you hold the patent for every mirror.
Your murderous form of self-defence
is an out-dated early warning system
plugged into cemented underground bunkers,
beyond all hope of renovation.
You are in this way the United States
at the logical end of its paranoia,
annihilating everything you touch
in your mission to ensure perpetual peace.
I will call you my own killing machine
and lay my body in front of your wheels.

Two Women and a Young Girl
at the Crawford Municipal Art Gallery, Cork[*]

She looks like my father's mother,
her hair neatly parted in the middle,
her daydream no doubt devotional,
head turned to the idea of God,
her hands held in the attitude of prayer,
though the left gently touches her cheek,
so that perhaps it is her husband
or her secret love that swells her eyelids
and runs through the sweet kiss-curl of her lips.
She sleeps in stone, dreaming of him,
united in her desire and hope,
flanked by the street-level poster-blonde
framed by the gallery window, who says:
time for a total revolution in image.
Above the active and passive heads
giant cranes are searching for tomorrow.

She looks out of the blackness,
the dark night of her mourning,
her red lipstick marking her youth,
the sexual devastation of her loss.
The beauty of her face is the thing,
the statement, symbol, the rebuke
to a world that still allows warfare
to burn love into the ashes of her sorrow.
She is untouched by time, radiant,
and stepping backwards into the abyss.

She looks beyond the goose on her lap,
far beyond the rural corner of her world,

---

[*] Seamus Murphy's 'Daydream' (1931), John Lavery's 'The
Widow' (1920), and Edith Somerville's 'The Goose Girl' (1888).

her innocent eyes, black as her hair,
fixed on the lifetime's hardships to come.
She looks down her allotted stretch of time,
her red lips mouthing the words she will speak
in self-defence, in desperation, in the heated
moment of the one passion she will know.
The goose looks away from its future,
she, with eyes on the verge of song, braves hers.

Evidence

The only photograph I have of you
is from a passport run of four,
one you didn't need to use
to effect your escape from me.

It lives within that memory box
and gets remembered every other year,
your face remaining beautiful
as the touch of your lips decays.

One day I will look at you
as an illustration in a book
I have no intention of purchasing
let alone desire to read.

One day you will be nothing more
than an image of temporary note
flashed before disinterested eyes
at an airport security check-in.

Dreamhole

For Sarah Wood

She said. That was her.
We must dream and dream
well, she said.
That was her
or was it him?
Sometimes she said her
and sometimes she said him.
She said
that they were abortive monsters,
our dreams,
or her dreams,
or his.
Who owns a quotation
when it's quoted?
That she didn't say
or ask.
But she said her
and she said him.
The enemy of immortality
is lodged within ourselves ....
That was a quotation.

I was sitting in a lecture hall,
colloquosphere,
listening to her,
Hélène Cixous,
say her
and say him,
next to my friend,
and others.

Nothing is eternal now,
and nothing ever was.
That was always true

and always will be true.
Forever.
And in dreams we know this.
This is perhaps
my friend's dreamhole,
as if the stars were tiny pinpricks,
peepholes,
for once not distant
but very close,
intimate today,
or the half-moon as it creeps
across a gap in night-clouds,
a tattered, worn place
in an almost blanket,
substitute canopy,
wanting and not wanting
to be seen,
or the sunspot in the hand,
the chest
or stomach,
that children make,
my children make,
her children make,
sleeping
or not sleeping.

Those radiant windows,
those chords
that are wounds,
those dreamholes,
they speak another golden world
of light and love
and seeing sight.
"We all give off light, Graham!"
she said to me.

I wrote a song about it once,
that infinite dancehall,

as I imagine —
First Corinthians Thirteen
and onwards,
Dante's giant disco ball,
ball within ball,
besides, between,
glitteroscopy,
light thrown and magnified
and understood
and seen.
I called it *Blind*.
It is very sad
and beautiful
and lost.
She will never hear me
sing it,
until then,
until there,
until him and her.

Later, alone,
I made a promise,
looking at that contemplative face,
slumbering,
wandering in dreams,
almost full,
it said this:
I will make a poem
out of every time we meet,
in dreams
or, simply,
dreaming.

A Night In with the Stars

There are no prizes for losers.
There are no losers when the prizes
are dished out, since
by the time the ceremony begins
and the first set of hairdos
waddle up to the illuminated microphone,
all the losers have gone home.
Some have no doubt taken taxis,
others, refusing to rush, have taken risks
with traffic, have walked through unlit
pedestrian precincts,
past dubious-looking, stationary men,
to watch the proceedings on television
and to celebrate, or at least witness,
how fame creates its own quarantine,
each gorgeous, spectral body, Beatrice-like,
a light reflecting light reflecting light
reflecting light, until
it becomes at least possible to consider
how the dolphins, knowing what way
the wind was blowing, decided
on one impossibly starry night,
after an implausibly protracted discussion,
to ditch their lumpen hooves,
to return to the oceans
and take their chances there.

Apparently, there is a dolphin myth,
made long ago, by the coast
of an as yet unilluminated America,
that the stars, which puncture
the otherwise blank and unassuming sky,
are the heads of other celestial dolphins,
curious, adventurous even,
and yet happy in their watery abode,
their own habitual constellations.

40

Anthropomorphism

It is far closer to the core
than the leaves blowing into
adjectives beyond the wind,
or anxious sheep considering
the spectral patterns
vapour trails smudge
against the cold November sky.
It is far more reluctant
to arrive than the sovereign,
medieval pageant
of insect, beast, or fowl,
the ancient divisions,
Queen, colony, tribe and tribute,
all undone, unfolded, all lost.
It speaks in the fall of a tree,
but not in the commerce
of the four lane, duplex
concourse of ants that succeeds.
Its tiniest, bird-like nuances
lie buried inside of what's forgotten.
Only the word decays
seems free of its corruption,
the bad mouth and reek of figure.
The fog does not creep, insinuate,
the hills are not quiet,
the oak and ash do not quiver,
or stand in secret concave.
There is no assembly of horses,
though they circle and nudge one another.
The field does not fizzle with frost.
Over the stark blue November
morning an orb shaped like the moon
neither glides nor looks away.

Modern Prometheus

That man is on fire.
In lurid blue, gold and red
he runs passed parked cars,
pedestrian children, a man
walking a small, black dog,
a bin with a grate for cigarette butts
on top, a triangulated placard
reading, "O'Brien's Leather Accessories",
and leaves a trail of mini-
explosions, small, random fires,
like an Olympic torch-bearer
propelled by destiny
declaring that today the Games
are open, everywhere.

That man is on fire.
He runs passed the hospital,
through the small municipal
green, setting plastic-bags,
rose-beds, and the occasional,
startled pensioner alight,
into the corner, newspaper
kiosk. The stacks of *Sunday Times*
are first to go. The contagion
spreads like a camera's pan-shot.
But he buys his broad-sheet,
charred and flaking in his
curious hands, and he reads.
Sparks fizz off his involuntary tears.

That man is on fire.
Inconsolable, sensible of danger,
a growing threat, he runs down
Central Street, already emptied,
Police and military stationed
in requisitioned vehicles, one

Hegarty crane and a local, council
refuge van, into the lift
that will take him to safety.
But the heat is too intense,
he cannot close the doors,
and he sees two snipers,
well positioned, and an uncovered
gas-pipe, neglected since last Christmas.

That man is on fire.
He walks, impenetrable,
out into the evaporating air,
the sun dimmed in his own wake,
and he finds himself in the resident's
car-park. His presence
is intolerable, vehicles erupt
into intermittent protest,
windscreens pop like flat Champagne.
He decides to sit and wait it out,
to leave the last word to his
hunters, an obscenity
without a plan, a man on fire
without hope, a burning question.

Think of the Earth

I could tell what she looked like
from the back of her head
and the way her loosely falling hair
traced continental patterns on her neck.
And she was as tall as a mountain,
Juno Moneta, maker of money,
witness of the eternal present,
sister-double of Mnemosyne,
the goddess of non-interventionism,
cruel, impassive voyeur of war.
The idea she might turn her face to meet me
was the apocalypse.

The only reason I ventured
within a million miles of her
was that I knew what Keats
had once known and said,
which is that poetry, truth, beauty,
call it what you will, lies hidden
somewhere within her desolate shadow,
aching for excavation and return.

Lacking his courage I asked
no questions, snuck by on the blind-side,
until I found the sentence
I'd been looking for, engraved
on a small volcanic stone
in tiny, feminine characters.
It was entirely understandable this time,
held none of its previous opacity.
I put it in my inside pocket and took it home,
determined to show it to others,
or at least bear witness to its possession.

Great Eastern

In the way in which trains reduce a lifetime
to a series of obstinate vistas,
the crooked spire at Chesterfield,
the snaking turn at Berwick-upon-Tweed,
Tay Bridge or sun-drenched erotic gherkin,
Highbury coming out of King's Cross,
so desire transforms our world
into a landfill of contingent objects,
me a desolate seagull
rummaging around for meaning,
you an unopened packet of sweets
I will search for but never find.

And now as the sun breaks through
clouds that have imprisoned it all morning,
and the trees come to life beyond Darlington,
I know that this is a world of lost chances
and cannot but regret I did not kiss you
during a half-lit summer night at Ullapool,
the silhouette sea lapping on the rocks,
the cliff-birds invisible, observant,
and explain why my desire for you
was as lonely as the Angel of the North.
The train slides into Newcastle Station
like a tape-cassette on rewind.

As we moved into Scotland
I thought I heard music,
something inhuman, aerial,
wafting over the pale blue water.
I was reading a book about gaps
and silences, about how, given time,
meaning seeps through the cracks,
and quite frequently does not.
Just before Kirkcaldy I remembered
how large the sky had appeared

in my inexperienced London eyes,
and what you once said about Plato:
"up here, you see, the sun's so low
you can look straight into it."
By Ladybank's fields of mist
night had captured all the higher hills.

Auctioneer

The plants, in the to-die-for house,
within the to-die-for living-room,
against the killer, ceramic wall,
are green, more than green,
in the way that he, posing,
has more than one heart,
a face that could print money,
clothes that softly hang
and cannot be bought by you,
a book that is also a statement.

Everything here speaks to itself:
Outside the automated windows
the sky is a blue you do not recognise;
the frameless, but colourful, print
above the unlit fireplace,
is iconic, if unfamiliar;
the expensive white sofa, positioned
at an optimum length for viewing
the unplugged flat-screen television,
is leather and has never been sat on.

Maybe there is more than silence.
Maybe he has arranged for music
or for the afternoon clatter
of children to ascend from below.
Maybe, in another part of the house,
a woman is quietly singing,
or filling an ostentatiously large
crystal bowl with shiny, black stones.
Perhaps a man in similar clothes,
concealed beneath a beige overcoat,
is standing outside the front door
of the house, attempting to lock it
as discretely as he can.

Indigestion

And so he took to writing poetry
during evening meal times,
a brown moleskin pad by his side
soiled by the indelible slops
of risottos, casseroles and soups.

He discovered the analogy between green beans
and the lonely wilds of the eastern steppe,
how fish made him sing of the stars,
and beef, slowly cooked in its own juices,
took him inside the loveliest of eyes.

The bitter connection between garlic and loss
lifted him into the realm of mourning.
At the end of every silent meal
a poem worthy of the name,
until one began that would not stop.

He asked his wife to cook only lentils,
but the stanzas and cantos served themselves up.
He sucked on stones, chewed on twigs,
but nothing plugged his narrative art.
He thought about starvation, and then about irony,

then about vocation, and eventually the gods,
and still the epic violence of his tongue
came spewing out as if at command,
an ugly song about poverty and greed
no one who wished for beauty could stand.

Distracted, he took himself to the cliffs
and, as the sun dipped its toes in the west,
gave himself to the ever hungry sea.

Passage

For Harold Bloom

i

And soon, there being no end,
he forgot how he had begun,
and could not tell
whether he was falling still
or rising.

ii

Why must there be this untutored clash,
this ever trumpeted division and discord?
Light and dark, east and west,
full moon and crescent, frost and fire,
you and I. I deny them all.
In the name of the light that separates itself
through imperfectly closed wooden blinds
only to blend together to form one ray,
one undeniable beam, I deny them all.
In the name of You and I, I deny them all.

iii

If I injure myself, is it for you?
If I neglect my body,
tighten my lip,
no longer point my face
towards what makes me happy;
if I burn myself by the water
or freeze my bones outside
of hearth and home,
do you think it is for you?

I have cut myself so badly
that I begin to feel.

iv

In the garden
he rose above himself
and paused.

He denied the intuition of the sun,
the elective demonstration of hills,
the simple pride of oak and lily.

He presumed there would be other days,
interrogative, challenged, somewhat straightened.
But he rose above himself on this day.

He paused.
In the garden, he said:
"This is enough. This is home."

v

If I were to have my days again
I would repeat the same mistakes:
the same enemies, the same misguided kisses,
the same unnoticed tragedies and triumphs.

If I were to have my days again,
knowing what acts were wise, and what unholy,
my hand would still reach out to you
and you would still crumble at its touch.

vi

And soon, there being no end,
he forgot how it had begun,
and could not tell
whether he was falling still
or rising.

Oireachtas Report

Those who have gone pile up
in the empty spaces, in their tens
and twenties, their hundreds
and their thousands, lap on lap,
shoulder to shoulder, staggering
pyramids of the accusing dead,
the barred, the exiled, the dispossessed
and the gunned down, all ghosts now,
see-through heroes and martyrs,
screaming at an obscene abnegation,

as six suits, dry-cleaned
for the cameras, point their glasses
and brightly coloured plastic wallets
at imaginary opponents on deserted seats.

Patrick's Street

Your new millennial tiles are cool
beneath the feet of floodlit winter shoppers.
Have you forgotten so quickly
how everything within you burned?

A Prayer

Ireland, beyond Kent Station, Cork,
land of mist and newly built houses,
birthplace of sheep and graveyard of tractors,
home of unused rail-track and distant hill fires,
where decommissioned school buses huddle in conversation
and monastery ruins wait in silence for the end,
where yards stacked with incendiary black rubber tires
and pre-96 motorcars eat up the rain
and field beyond field of unslaughtered cattle
tilt their heads, unconscious, and ironically chomp,
like a train's disembarked slow-moving queue
of commuters and sight-seers hug their mobile phones.
Ireland, beyond Kent Station, Cork,
continue to resist me and my quest for a home.

The Fags

One day I will give up smoking,
one day, before it becomes too late
and I have lost my chance to be
my father, emerging as if by magic,
out of a rush-hour crowd of commuters,
at Liverpool Street Station
on a Friday afternoon, at the peak
of summer, his shirt-collar open,
his jacket slung across his shoulder,
his grin like a celebrity's greeting,
the sun pouring out of his eyes,
the hero of a thousand well-told stories,
a year or two before final retirement,
looking like a man anyone would marry,
carrying his Torygraph, the crosswords
finished, under his free left arm,
a baton, or that truncheon he returned
and that I coveted as a relic,
blithe escapee from a thousand
close-shaves, freedom in his face
and mischief in his eyes, Israel
and Ireland shooting through his mind,
as he cuts through the crush like parted
waves, Moses, incognito, within
the Promised Land, and mistakes me,
his own Telemachus,
for an obstacle in his singular career.

Revenant

After Joyce

At the first turn of the road
I looked back; she wasn't there,
she'd gone in, to sleep maybe,
maybe to put her hair in place,
for the sake of her husband,
expected from Cobh.
She didn't mean, no, she didn't
mean what I thought she did.
A woman like that, in her own
home, would never want
the likes of me, not at all,
not with my foreign airs,
the still-born vowels
in my London tongue,
a man with the kind of history
that's written on my face.
No, she didn't mean, not at all.

At the first turn of the road
I looked back and saw her,
standing, lovely, a picture
in her white night gown.
I must confess I tried my eyes
to see if it was see-through.
It took me I've no notion
how long
before I turned myself,
my longing gaze,
to the inferno of her cottage
and then back, with her,
screaming something,
her mouth opening
and closing,
like a strange fish,

or barn-door banging,
the torch tight in her hand.

How could I go on
or, strange word, *return*?

Lago Trasimeno

i.m. Denise Scott, 1933 – 2013

Stranieri

I brought the Shelleys bound to these shores,
carried Blake in a small, black rucksack,
returned Vico, gave long overdue Livy back.

Each year the same self-customized,
checked-in library, repetitious to
campeggio, unique to me, if not to us.

I grow fond of all the strange hands, in futuro,
who will open books at cut-price prices
to find well preserved, alien bodies.

Lago Trasimeno

There is no rain here.
The river has dropped again
and we swim only because last winter
they thought to dredge the lake.
The hills are unchanged;
my favourite Botticelli hump
still evidences
the resolution life derives from art.
We have tried to sail
but the wind dies as soon
as it announces itself
and we end up resentful,
tired of chasing a force that collapses
and finally betrays its own promise
to take us from shore.

One day we will sail away,
you and I,
into the perfect hills of our choice,
the south side of our lake ever distant,
an unbreakable, indivisible round,
the sky above us a perfect blue,
as we imagined,
the necessity of weather,
the influence of others,
the anxious drizzle of futurity,
receding, as we speed along,
beyond the realms of Aeolus,
into a landscape that never changes,
discovered and realized
by our homesick hearts.

Others, perhaps, will look for us.
Between the wall,
where the water stops,
and the hills

and the cloud-terraced sky beyond,
their eyes will sweep,
searching for a clue,
across the entire lake,
as if it were a painting
by a master with a master's hand.
But they will not find us.
Only a poet, with a poet's eye,
will see and, in seeing,
understand.

After the Storm

Life calms down at Lago Trasimeno
to the sound of a solitary mosquito,
boats softly head-butting their moorings,
bachelor cicadas in high-rised pines
and the occasional secreted, puffed-up frog
mimicking the songs of mythical birds,
so that it can almost seem that the words
written here are some kind of addition
to the peace of the scene, after a storm,
at half-past-two, under emergent Umbrian stars,
as life returns to its noisy business.
But they are not and they never could be
and the inherited notion of being,
or presence or oneness is as vain
an ambition to nurture
or propagate as the hope of catching sight
of the mosquito, the very boat, or boats,
the insistent cricket, the Louis
Armstrong frog, the bolt of lightning,
in the very moment of their singular expression.

This is a world of indications, of afterings,
for you a world of signs merely, to which
you can make but observation and witness,
like a painter lovingly paints a landscape
he knows he will never inhabit,
or a face he will neither spit at nor kiss,
or a self-portrait he can only contrive
because of this bar on doing and being.
So write it down here as best you can,
your testimony, your foreign function,
that after the storm of August 2nd,
2011, those creatures that survived
and all the metallic and wooden bulk

of this orchestrated place,
resumed what work they had separately left off
with what seemed to you like deliberation.

Beyond Livy

i

The storm fizzes and crackles
in your brain, as you scatter
back to your flammable shack,
your mind full of current and full of Barca,
the chosen one, storm-maker,
sweeping down from out of the Alps.
He was a man who made the weather,
spreading violence out of his lips, his eye,
unimaginable, god-like,
to scholars, poets, and other men
who retreat, cower and wait for death,
instantaneous vaporisation,
and can barely understand
the common soldier's unbroken line,
their willingness to face the fire.
At Saguntum, for example,
they pushed on without him, the enemy's
hot spears whizzing past their heads.

ii

Livy, on the second wave, gives the details:
victories, defeats, standoffs, politics,
encampments, a list of comically
demotic omens, sky-crack, a hand,
a dazzling fork. There are
no sides in the aftermath, Scipio
Junior no agent of hope,
no new modernity, this side
of the lago's dirty wall. Barca
and all his pissed-up elephants
is no hero to me, who twitches
at the furthest, muted rumble. I want
what he thought and what he wrote
years after he declined to enter
Rome, declining years of non-
existence everything that was left
to own. What did he drink? What smoke?
What dream? What lago did he despair on?

iii

Poetry is at war with history.
It's sad, but it's true. It has to be.
No matter how you turn or twist it
science gives way to sympathy
and that won't stretch beyond these hills,
unless it's coloured by today,
our trivial, frivolous inconsequence.
Knowledge is what gets drunk and eaten.
Carthaginian, Roman, Celto-Iberian,
who are these people to you or me?
Life begins and ends as a wave
sucked up and spit out by the trees.
La Repubblica posts a series every decade,
but the facts of the matter, if you want them, are this:
the lake once stretched to Cortona and beyond
and once was a tiny pond in a ditch;
the hills have grown by half an inch
since smarty-pants beat his neighbour at chess.

iv

"I bore my exile patiently,"
Dryden translates, assisted
by eminent hands. Twenty thousand
or more, lost within the icy peaks,
fifteen thousand drowned, beheaded,
by Trasimene's shores, at Cannae
the unprecedented rout,
outdoing the Somme, outdoing number.
"Patiently." One would need something more,
something like guilt, regret, revelation.
I would take enlightenment,
the slow, steady comprehension
that life is life and death is death
and intervention for the gods alone,
not for the likes of you or me
or men who enter god look-alike contests.
The bin Laden of his generation,
learning to accept the necessity of love.

v

Storming Norman confessed,
though it's uncertain he was citing
Livy. Cannae was
his blueprint, ancient model,
his thin blue line intertext,
sucking in the greater strength,
like a snake consumes a dog
or horse, outflanking swelling
pride as a womb, suffocating force
with bitter caresses. But he omits
the final chapter of the day,
the afterword and epilogue,
the hard, bloody, liquid labour,
where no foot can stand
and the ground begins to melt and
gag on its super-sized feed
of bone and blood, and the corporals
mutter, "will this ever be over?"

vi

There are no modern prodigies,
no babies born with elephant heads,
no rain of milk or blood or stones,
no double sun or triple moon,
no cows speaking Latin or Greek,
no altars sweating, no temples cracked
and splintered into jigsaw pieces,
no trees sucked into the earth
or ships flung out of the ocean,
no surprise androgynous sheep,
no inexplicable fires in the sky,
no unaccountable rumble at dawn,
no hiss and steam at dusk.
Fortune is out of favour
and we fight corporate wars
for justice, freedom, democracy,
without mystery, without sacrifice,
without hope of reparation.

vii

I see one anachronistic bullet,
defying time, space, and logic,
the separate chapters, the separated
events of his narration. One magic
bullet retelling the story
of how violence begets violence,
making Barca half-blind as it rips
through his face, scything down,
as from machine guns, uncontrollable
elephants refusing to ford
the bloody Metaurus, severing
the brother's head from the brother's
shoulders, before it pops, like a seed
pressed from that much loved nose,
and slams, with unprecedented force,
into the very idea of Carthage.
This is the bullet, originally shot from Eden,
that one day will murder history.

viii

Periochae, Book Thirty Five,
on how things have not changed,
the masculine habit of fishing
going on and on and on and on:
if Alexander first, then who second?
if Pyrrhus second, then who third?
if Barca third, then who fourth?
The answer is simple and runs like this:
not you! Whatever way we turn this,
never you! The game, it is a game,
is called Hostility, Perpetual Warfare,
and it is played without end,
being a game without end
or any possibility of resolution,
for the sake of the bubble of ephemeral
names: Generals, Kings, Warriors,
Heroes, bobbing up and then collapsing
like balls in a frenzied bingo hall.

ix

And he omits also
the full lesson and consequence
of Cannae, and every other
famous victory, the famous
victory revenged. All famous
victories are revenged, sooner
or later, sometimes themselves
with famous victories. So that
revenge and defeat double backward
into victory, and one forgets,
Rome having crumbled into ruin,
Carthage nothing but a textbook name,
who won the ultimate, conclusive
battle, who came out on top
in the final reckoning.
The pride of his academy,
Stormin' Norman knew no doubts
as he made his dash for God and country.

X

How could he not have had a plan,
beyond vague notions of empire
and honour, and a promise made
in childhood to please the father?
Maharbal was right. In the fallout,
after the deadly, double embrace,
the corpse-trail from New Carthage
rose to a peak in stunned Apulia,
where ghosts wander in search of their limbs
and, every morning, still plead for release.
It's true! The gods did not fill
one vessel with all available gifts,
and in their wisdom, or their wit,
remain inscrutable on certain points,
questions recurrent at Ypres, Ho Chi Minh
City, Basra. Such as, what possible
use? and, still sounding in our ears,
how could he not have had a plan?

xi

Juvenal's terminal signet-ring
links more than Barca's suicide
with the countless fingers of Cannae's
dead. Considering Xerxes arrives,
setting out on a miracle flotilla
only to return on a sea
of corpses, and since Alexander
links his bloody name between
these paragons of vain ambition,
and considering the fact
that he omits to mention Pyrrhus
and Scipio Africanus, and that
we might anachronistically add
Boney, Wellington, Rommel, Monty,
and many more monumental cognomes
in the roll-call of premeditated
slaughter, it should not be necessary
to underscore the meaning of that ring.

xii

Scipio learnt what Hannibal knew,
civilisation takes over from nature,
so that men learn to become the weather
and strike like lightning out of the hills.
And nature is necessary,
so that Rome can presume its right
to roll like verdure over the world.
Remember, though, he was no pharmakos,
knocked up only to be knocked down.
He was the unappeasable nightmare
every new Rome must repress,
something unpleasant to swallow,
suck down into untried guts,
the most unpalatable medicine known.
And he is at the Colline Gates,
call him the Gulf Stream shutting down
or tens of millions dispossessed.
At bedtime repeat: *Hannibal ad portas!*

xiii

When troops are shifted across the globe
in locust numbers, and the big guns
and the newly shaped ships are lifted
out of the dockyards and factories
of the world. When women return
to their household gods, neglected
during times of peace, and wives
and mothers leave their work to spend
all day by the shrines and inside chapels,
when tanks begin to patrol the streets
of those who have given up their sons
and daughters to the great cause
of God-knows-what, and politicians
grin and speak of sacrifice
and eventual liberation,
and everything is necessary
and nothing makes sense, then whisper
to your sleepy children, *Hannibal ad portas!*

Those Feet

William Blake put his foot in it.
He knew there were three portals to the stars
and that modern man had imprisoned one,
the ladies, except in private, all.
So he ran around his garden naked,
unlike Wordsworth owned no Wellingtons,
and lifting his legs up to the heavens
would call on Jehovah to come to heel.
There was more poetry in his one big toe
than ten thousand obedient Christian feet.
The foot-soldier that brought him up to law
was blind in his boots, his hands and his face.

He never made it to Italy,
the sunny home of barbaric art,
never got himself past Sussex,
made the Messiah walk all that long way home.
But I see him here, sometimes,
wandering over the soft, green hills,
talking with angels at Magione,
swimming with children, saving lives,
debating with soldiers on Tuoro's height,
explaining to Flaminius, in great detail,
why the chickens wouldn't breakfast that morning,
the reason why the battle was always lost,
lamenting technological inventions:
the chariot, the motorcar, and the shoelace.

To Geoffrey Hill, Lago Trasimeno, July 2011

Reading the Pindarics of "our best poet",
mournful vitalist, on a day of drizzle
and threatening storms from the north,
stuck on the shop-front of our casetta,
I say I'd like to write like that, to a friend
who is no friend, so where the best friends are,
heart-gorge of discriminating division,
as in my own small way I have for you, so that,
I also say poems should be difficult,

like the greatest hearts and minds are gifted,
along life's purgatorial strait, and yet,
and this is where we differ, Geoff, not having met,
though naïf luxuriants told me to knock,
bold as brass, decades back, "If you feel that way!",
skirting Cambridge, but not so boldly
as to knock you down. Consternation, retreat,
defile of the beaten soul, something we share,
but separately vocalize. You would, I know,

no greater knowledge, already have turned,
in unsurpassable formal lines, sad trionfi
of unswollen tongue, the one that eludes me here
and I most want, Livy giving everything but
poetical eyes: Barca, the weather, living on.

Ba'al

No one is lighting
camp fires around the lago,
save the sun itself.

That crescent of death
from Passignano westward,
where I place myself.

Cottrell presents him
as much Greek as Phoenician,
so prototypic.

Elephant meat is
best served cold with a little
pepper and garlic.

A bow, an arc, sem-
i-circle, a scythe of hills.
Perfect killing fields.

The sun is so hot
it could fire a billion
dark satanic mills.

Two little witches
getting burnt alive, hissing
about stranieri.

As if they owned it,
the wall by the lago, what
we call Dún Laoghaire.

Like a minor god
mistakes himself for someone
who makes the weather.

You should learn correct
usage, for example, a
ba'al of white feathers ....

The sun has become
an Emperor we would all
like to see retire.

They feel no distress,
armour-plated as they are,
chariots of fire.

You would not want to
be out in this heat without
some strong protection.

Perfect for someone
with his eye in, the top half
of a huge question.

Tumbling downwards out
of the sky, because he fan-
cied what wasn't his.

I do here confess
that the quote about the saint
is Mussolini's.

Fallen pine needles.
You need never be in need
of a book marker.

His pupil swam like
a lottery ball, before
you know its number.

In the end, my friend,
whatever you say, the sun
will rise tomorrow.

He says thirty-six
thousand were lost between New
Carthage and the Po.

Invasion of heat,
life is difficult, la bo-
la Africana.

The lake and the hills
will one day be under un-
forgiving water.

The fiery cowhorns
at Campagna delivered
a fresh shadow cull.

Whenever the blue
of the sky is not the sky,
then you're in trouble.

If they had poets
they would be Modernists, man-
ifestoes blazing.

And there was the big
flagpole stuck fast in the mud.
But it's the chickens!

Two years ago, Vi-
co, in a summer full of
appropriate storms.

The brood of lions,
but with only one lion
amongst those lions.

Do not mistake me
for one minute, I think all
minutes come and go,

so, as in Nietzsche,
there is always return and
never. Capito?

Byron was clever.
If he is Manfred, then A-
starte brings in Ba'al.

O yes! Flamini-
us, ill-fated Consul, fell
off his animal.

They are less complex
in their adoration, one
could call it blind faith.

And if linked with Ba'al
then linked with fertility,
not tacky disgrace.

The wide-spread primi-
tive Semitic root may be
rendered as possess.

A nice little twist
for proto-Victorian
gentlemen to miss.

There is one sun god.
There is only one sun god.
There is one son god.

How the goodies are
turned bad, the baddies good, he,
Blake, well understood.

His family name is
proleptic, rather strange and
uncanny prequel.

So that the harvest
becomes an American's
idea of evil.

It amounts to fear.
It amounts to phobia.
I reject lightning!

Every net woven,
every trap that's sprung, he falls
out of everything.

She seems to believe
all the spiders in the world
are out to get her.

For all the 'serras,
ciaos and salves, there's enough
tension in the air.

Dictionaries, lexi-
cons, do not possess him now.
He fell out of them.

As if there had been
some kind of spidery vote,
spiderposium.

I imagine him
as relinquishing love, but
relishing his grub.

And a force that wants
to defeat death is labelled
as Beelzebub.

Remember one thing,
this comes from the lake, acqua
impotabile.

He seems to have thought
that his mere presence would win
complete loyalty.

We are prisoners.
It's so hot that everyone
hides inside their house.

Agricultural cult-
ure, afraid of famine and
Africa's locusts.

So that the blue sky
would be like the lago, on-
ly on top of us.

More alarming still,
fertility is not in
the lap of the gods.

And their poetry,
it would sting, a slap in the
face of public taste.

The lago knows what
to do with bodies, it man-
ages human waste.

You'd watch where you sit
down and put a beer mat on
your gin and ton-tons.

Was the promise made
in winter-time or summer?
The classic question.

Because I worry
that sun worship has survived
and strangely lingers.

The lake is a soup,
ba'al of mud, heated water
and sharpened fingers.

They say thirty-six
degrees, but some have told me
it's got to forty.

I want cessation,
I want finality. I'm
un-naturale.

Ashtoreth or A-
starte, equivalent to
Greek Aphrodite.

If I could shed my
skin in imitation of
scandalous Lord B.

There was a poem
about Emmanuelle,
but it didn't fit.

We are being cooked
and we get cross, sausages
beginning to spit.

Babylonian
bel can include ownership
over human beings.

Stand at Puntabell-
a and contemplate the sense
of life's ironies.

The weather man's face
droops, domaini e dopo-
domaini, caldo!

Since if you add in
a touch of Homer, he be-
comes transitional.

He starts as the sun
and then becomes mud and then
he is born again.

I will never say:
what we need is a storm, what
we need is some rain!

Sorry Professor,
was that thunderer or a
pun on the word boat?

Is it so foolish
to want to read those texts he
apparently wrote?

…. is a white-feathered
bird, one might imagine an
everyday chicken.

Lumps the shape if not
the size of the lago is
why we all flick them.

Ba'al of terror, fear
and anxiety. Ba'al of
insane projection.

The heat warps every-
thing, nothing can be straightened,
life is clinamen.

Yahweh takes over
on Mount Carmel from the god
who defeated mud,

but where's the god who
will finally defeat the
god of human blood?

Bottles pop, colour
fades away, everything is
trying to escape.

It's too hot to think,
to remember ancient myths,
that specific date.

If I was smarter
I'd link Barca's defeat and
Dido's desertion.

It would appear that
history is to blame, that's
the only version.

If you want to see
what he saw in the place, go
to Sanguineto.

Some local critic
has blacked out the "bor" in the
street sign "Borghetto".

When it came it took
us by surprise and hit us
all below the belt.

The sky cracked open
and something told me this is
how the Romans felt.

I watched as children
ran for cover and a wind
roared down from the trees.

I was jumping like
a jack-in-the-box, at each
new catastrophe.

It may be narci-
ssistic, but I do believe
that one will find me.

When it came I jumped
out of my skin into a
nearby zanzare.

I buzzed around new-
ly opened windows, freshness
returning from flood,

trying to remem-
ber something about war, storm,
Hannibal and blood ....

trying to remem-
ber, remember, remember,
something about mud ....

Hung Over

Last night the moon was just another lamp,
a sleeping face with large bruised eyes
posted on a flagpole, just above the trees,
one of a row of insect-breeding lights.
Around the lake you could hear the boom
of Domenica's late-night jollities,
camp drums demanding more drink, more flesh,
a general desire to forget domani.
I stayed for a while on the wall, face to face,
conscious that it looked less like slumber than death.
In the morning, stuck fast, it was in a state,
dropped into a sky of murky water,
dissolving, slowly losing its edges,
like a huge, yellowish, headache tablet.

Zanzare

i

Middle Italy playing dead, as it does at night,
leaving everything up to the insect world,
the half-drunk cups of Limoncello
and dregs of cheap red plonk
are being stormed by platoons
of kamikaze mosquitoes,
instantaneously drunk and dead
in their ageless version of suicide-bombing,
each one no doubt already intoxicated
on the idea of the eternal fat lands,
a celestial city of blood and dormant bodies
and an inexhaustible, radiant light
that does not move or mysteriously vanish,
welcoming, sublime, and above all cool.
If one could reason with them
the temptation would be to explain
that there are more effective methods
for ridding the world of its parasites.

ii

I sat among them as they died,
the zanzare and the vespe
and all other winged creatures
lower down the food chain than the bees,
drinking undiluted Gordon's gin
as they fell, plummeted, stormed upwards
on one last flight, or twirled, desperately,
on their backs, in an agony of dying.
I sat among the Guernica of insects,
half-an-hour after the motorized purge,
falsetto chainsaws and minute cushioned
table thuds rippling my stream of thought,
insecticide replacing oxygen,
as I struggled to find an appropriate conceit
for the extermination of small, genocidal species.
I was not a witness, I was happy in the cull,
save for the sheer, bloody inconvenience.

iii

This place fits the man who must flit.
Light and shade, visible, invisible,
a day of storm, a day of peace,
the lago violent, the lago placid,
more happiness than he could ever enjoy,
terror streaking the early evening dark.
That most saintly of all saintly men
still found doubt on Isola Maggiore.

I cannot make this place symphonic,
calm after stress after opening sweetness.
"Next year, we must get down before Agosto!"
A boat capsizes near San Feliciano,
the children dance to old Euro hits.
Cena echoes with joy and sorrow.

Blake's "Ghost of a Flea", dictated to Varley,
keeps returning and returning to notice;
angry men, hungry for blood,
reduced to a reproducible size,
caught in a vortex of divine justice,
which could not cope if they were any larger.

Last night, in the after-storm coda,
released back into the viali,
I heard them in their re-born billions,
humming, above the trees, like electricity.
They own this place in their small cycle
of birth, blood, satiety and fall.
They know another storm is coming,
just like the others, dopo and before.

iv

I keep flicking them
with my fingers, as if they
were Subbuteo players.
Little men, one goal in mind,
me a goalkeeper.

V

I wonder, as they freeze dry,
legs becoming plinths,
or ditch life, sting upwards,
in one last defiant gesture,
our Umbrian table,
in the dead of night,
a map of the world
that should be included
in the Vatican's map room,
whether they revert,
overpowered by passion,
anger zapping through them,
at last! to human recollection?

I sit here, year after year,
meditative, scripting
poem after poem, so
I do not become one.

Autunno

There are no more visions here.
The uomini-ombra have packed up
and gone. Ferragosto is a memory.
Soon the evenings will be more
than chilly, the lago silent,
save for itself. The local fishermen
and foreign fishermen are already
laying down watery carpets, this year's
thoros, ready for next summer's
metaphysical catch. The Perugians
are following suit, boxing up porcelain
coffee sets, securing wooden shutters,
driving their children away,
sweeping up leaves as if all the leaves
had already fallen.

But listen, and believe,
this is no time for departure,
this is a time worth waiting for,
forgotten and forgetful. Anything
that bites now will be real.

Lightning Source UK Ltd.
Milton Keynes UK
UKOW03f0915310314

229131UK00001B/5/P